OUR ENDANGERED EARTH

DAVID COOK
ENVIRONMENT

CONTENTS

CROWN PUBLISHERS INC. NEW YORK

The environment

If you travel to different parts of the world, you will see different forms (or species) of plant and animal life. This is because all living things have changed to fit in with their surroundings. And as the world is very varied, the plants and animals in it are also very diverse. They have adapted to their natural habitat, but are unable to thrive in other parts of the world, where conditions are different.

The environment is the name given to everything which affects the life of a plant or animal in its immediate surroundings. This includes the climate, the soil and water, and also the other plants and animals living in the area.

Climate is an important factor. Animals from a cold climate cannot survive in the tropics, and tropical animals perish in a cold climate. Many plants die if they are moved

The diagram shows very simply how a life cycle works in a forest environment. The squirrel finds food from the tree and the fox eats the squirrel. When animals or plants die, they decompose and enrich the soil. This helps the tree to grow, and so continue the life cycle.

Tundra

The land around the Arctic Ocean is called a tundra. Snowbound for most of the year, no trees can grow there. Only a few animals, like the musk ox, live there all year round.

Coniferous forests

Coniferous forests grow where long cold winters give way to brief hot summers. Only the coniferous trees can withstand this climate. Squirrels are typical animals there.

Temperate forests

Temperate forests grow where both summers and winters are less extreme. Many of the trees shed their leaves in autumn, but enough food can still be found to feed the deer in winter.

Grasslands

Grasslands are found on wide plains in both tropical and temperate areas where rainfall is insufficient for trees to grow. Fleet-footed grazers, like the horse, are typical.

somewhere unfamiliar to them.

Water and soil also make up an important part of the environment. No life can exist without water. In the case of plants, the amount of water available to them depends not only on rainfall, but also on the type of soil. Water drains through some soils very rapidly, giving plants little time to catch it. Another type of soil retains water, but sun or wind may dry out the surface. So, in order to survive, plants have had to adapt to growing in the special conditions dictated by their environment.

Animal life is closely linked with plant life, because plants form the basis of the food chain. Some animals, called herbivores, eat plants, while others, called carnivores, kill the herbivores for food, or feed off their carcasses. But none of these animals could survive without plants. For instance, the zebra eats grass, and the lion eats zebras, so without grass, both the zebra and the lion would die out because there would be nothing for either to eat.

The land can be divided into a number of regions, called realms, according to the different plant life in each. Six of the eight realms exist in specific geographical parts of the world. These are the tundra, coniferous forests, temperate woodlands, grasslands, deserts and tropical forests. Two more realms, mountains and inland waters, are scattered throughout the world.

Each realm is home to many animals which have adapted to living there. Humans are the only species able to live all over the world. This is because we can change the environment to suit our needs. Unfortunately, when we do this, we often destroy many plants and animals living there.

Tropical forests

Tropical forests grow where rainfall is high. Trees grow swiftly and can flower or fruit at any time in the year. Most animals, like the monkey, are adapted to living in trees.

Deserts

Deserts are found where rainfall is too low to support much plant life. Both plants and animals, such as the camel, have adapted to survive long periods without water in the desert.

Inland waters

Inland waters range from great lakes and rivers to tiny ponds and streams. A great variety of life is found in fresh water. Beavers make their homes in streams, rivers and lakes.

Mountains

Mountains cover one fifth of the world's land. Animals, like the ibex, have adapted to the harsh conditions found there including thin air, cold, and scant vegetation.

Humans

As part of the animal kingdom, humans are mammals belonging to the order of primates, which includes monkeys and apes. We are the most successful species on earth. Our population is vast compared to any other species of large mammals, and the only others which approach our numbers are our own domestic animals.

Although we are part of nature, we have developed skills which have set us apart from the rest of the natural world. We can record information and pass on our knowledge for future generations to build on. Largely because of this unique ability, we have taken a new course in evolution. Rather than changing physically in order to fit in with our environment, we have changed the world to suit our needs.

Human society has progressed rapidly and dramatically, yet our physical appear-

These mammoth-hunters lived in Russia 20,000 years ago. They were not restricted to living in a warm climate, because they had learned to make fire, clothes and shelter.

Farming began about 10,000 years ago. Wheat and barley, reaped with flint sickles, were the main crops (below). Farming allows people to settle and their numbers to grow, for land used this way can support many. Now farms provide the food for all of us.

Farming settlements were once tiny areas in the wilderness (right). But we now cultivate all suitable land. In many places small woods and hedgerows provide the last refuges for wild life (below right). But even these are threatened by modern farming practices.

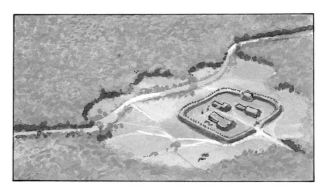

ance has changed very little. Given a haircut, a shave and a modern suit, a man who lived thirty thousand years ago would look no different from a modern man. But our way of life is very different from that of our ancestors, and the effect we have had on the living world is profound.

Ten thousand years ago humans wandered the earth in small groups, making temporary shelters for themselves, hunting wild animals and gathering plants. But then people learned to farm the land, and changed the world. At first, progress was slow and the damage done was slight.

But over the last five hundred years the human population has exploded, and we have transformed the earth. We have built cities, roads and factories. We have become so powerful that we can control what grows in fertile land, and we can change or destroy habitats in most areas of the world.

The changes we make to the landscape can have far-reaching effects. Soil, climate, plants and animals make up a delicate natural balance, and radical changes disturb or even destroy that balance.

In the course of our success as a species, we have destroyed a great deal of life around us. A long list of animals and an enormous number of plants have already become extinct as a result of our actions. In fact, it is thought that many unknown plants are dying out even before we have had time to discover them. Fertile land has been changed into dust bowls, and grasslands into deserts. But while we change nature to suit our own purposes, we also rely on it for the resources we need in order to survive. We need to preserve the natural world, not only for the wild plants and animals, but for ourselves, too.

Machines have given us the power to change the world more swiftly than was possible when people used only their muscles, and the help of their working animals, like oxen and horses.

Modern technology enables us to make many things we think we need. But an unwelcome effect of industry is the pollution it can create.

The cold north

The polar region extends across the far north of America, Europe and Asia, and is one of the most inhospitable environments for life on earth.

The tundra, which surrounds the Arctic Ocean, is a vast treeless wilderness, frozen for much of the year. The sun is only seen for six months, and during the long dark winters few animals live there. These include the rare musk oxen and large numbers of lemmings which provide food for the Arctic foxes and stoats.

But in the brief summer, plants burst into life and vast numbers of birds and animals visit the tundra to take advantage of this short season of plenty. The caribou of North America migrate there, followed by the wolves which prey on them. They return to the coniferous forests in winter.

Immediately south of the tundra, there are coniferous forests which encircle the world. Trees can grow here because the winters are milder and the summers longer. The cone-bearing evergreens provide food for many insects and a few birds, such as the grouse and crossbill. Hunters like sables and martens, live in the forests. These prey on pine-eating red squirrels, chipmunks and flying squirrels. The forests are dotted with marshes and lakes where caribou and moose congregate.

Neither the tundra nor the coniferous forests are suitable for agriculture because the climate is too cold and the soil is infertile and ill-drained.

However, the polar regions have long been a source of luxury furs, and animals such as beavers, sables, minks and silver foxes have been mercilessly hunted.

The coniferous forests have a long history as the world's prime source of timber, and vast quantities of trees are felled every year. As the cleared land cannot be farmed, new trees can grow, and no permanent damage

gyrfalcon

musk ox

snowy owl

stoat (ermine)

Arctic fox

Arctic lemming

ptarmigan

Arctic hare

Tundra residents
These animals can survive on the tundra all the year round, living on the frozen vegetation or preying on each other.

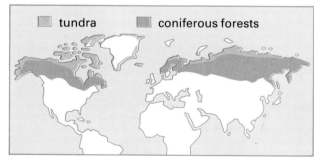

tundra   coniferous forests

is done. But modern technology has now brought the threat of pollution.

Pulp mills deposit sawdust into the rivers, and in large enough quantities it could affect the fish and other animals living in the water. Trees on the southern fringes of the forest are being sprayed with insecticides, and there is some danger that these poisonous chemicals will affect other animals.

The discovery of minerals and oil is an added threat. The mines and oil wells, together with recently established military bases, mean that the region is becoming more populated. More people with guns are coming into the area, and casual shooting is an increasing threat.

But, modern industry need not destroy wildlife. For example, an overground pipeline runs from Alaska to North America, cutting across the caribou migration routes. But special bridges and underground passes have been built to allow the caribou to migrate safely. At first, it was feared that the animals might not use the passes, but in fact they have, and this is one encouraging example of successful conservation.

Summer visitors
Many birds visit the tundra to breed there but return south in the winter.

red-breasted goose

sandhill crane

eider duck

moose

caribou

flying squirrel

pine marten

red squirrel

spruce grouse

wolf

crossbill

grizzly bear

wolverine

All these animals shelter in the forests during the winter but many of them migrate to the tundra in the brief summer there.

Forest dwellers
Squirrels, grouse and crossbills live on pine shoots and cones. These never leave the forest. Neither do pine martens which prey on them.

Temperate forests (1)

Most temperate forests are made up of trees which grow leaves in the spring and summer and shed them in the autumn.

They are found in temperate climates, where summers are warmer and winters milder than in coniferous zones. The largest areas of temperate forest are found in the northern hemisphere, across Europe, North America and Asia, but there are also some smaller areas of temperate forest south of the equator.

The mild climate, frequent rainfall and fertile soil of these forests provide ideal conditions for a rich variety of vegetation and animal life. In the northern temperate woodlands, the leaf mold under the trees is the home of numerous small rodents such as voles and mice, as well as animals like shrews and hedgehogs, which eat worms and insects. Predators include owls, hawks and foxes. Large plant-eaters, such as deer, live here, as do the wolves and lynx which prey on them. Squirrels and chipmunks nest in the trees, and bats roost in the hollows.

The temperate forests also attract many birds. Some, like woodpeckers, live there all the year round and feed off grubs in the bark of the trees. Others, such as fly catchers and warblers, migrate there in the summer to take advantage of the abundant insect life. In winter, when there are no insects, they return to warmer lands.

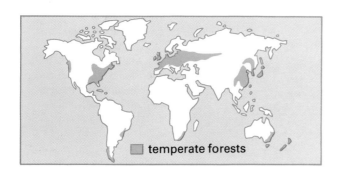

temperate forests

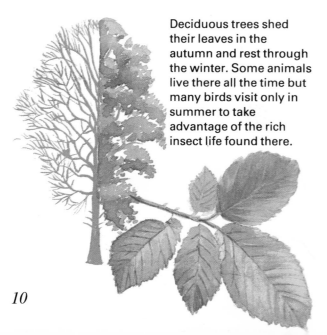

Deciduous trees shed their leaves in the autumn and rest through the winter. Some animals live there all the time but many birds visit only in summer to take advantage of the rich insect life found there.

red squirrel

pied flycatcher

badger

red fox

rabbit

The annual fall of leaves in temperate forests enriches the soil, so that when the trees are cut down the land can be turned into fertile farmland. For this reason, temperate forests have been altered more than any other natural habitat in the world. In south-east China, for instance, the forests have been so completely destroyed that no remnant survives today. In Europe, the process has been less radical, but even so, only tiny patches of the original forests remain. During the last two thousand years they have been almost completely replaced by farms, towns and cities. However, the changes to the European landscape have been gradual enough to enable most animals to adapt. For example, forest birds and animals have adapted to living in hedgerows and waste land.

But the larger wild animals have been less successful. Two European mammals, the wild ox (or auroch), and the tarpan, a wild horse, have become extinct. The European bison only narrowly escaped the same fate. Wolves, exterminated long ago in Britain, now only survive in a few remote corners of Europe. Lynxes and wild cats are also rare.

Deer and wild boar still live in Europe because they have been protected as game animals since the Middle Ages. Today, some are protected in nature reserves, but many more are protected to provide sport.

purple emperor

red deer

wild boar

hedgehog

wood warbler

Woodland life
The picture shows some of the variety of forest life. All these animals can live together without directly competing with each other for food or territory.

Wolves and bears, which used to prey on wild pigs and deer, are no longer found in the woodlands of Europe. Now the pigs and deer need only fear the hunter.

There are still many small rodents and birds in the woodlands, together with their predators, such as hawks, foxes, stoats and badgers.

Temperate forests (2)

Europe now has very little truly unspoiled land, and so wild animals are mainly confined to small areas of woodland and heath, patches of uncultivated land, hedge-rows and roadside greenery

But in recent times even these last refuges have been invaded. Hedgerows are being ripped out so that huge agricultural machines can work efficiently in large fields. Even when hedges are simply trimmed, giant cutters called flails are often used, and these dislodge many birds' nests.

Roadside greenery is often cleared in order to give motorists a good view of the road ahead. The use of herbicide, or weed-killer, is a cheap and easy method of clearing the areas, but many rare plants and flowers die in the process.

On farmland, pesticides are used to control pests harmful to crops, but butterflies and other insects are also killed. Pesticides are dangerous to birds, too. If a bird eats enough poisoned berries or insects it will die. Bigger predatory birds can then be poisoned by eating the meat of an affected bird. Hawks became rare because insecticides in their systems caused them to lay thin-shelled eggs which broke easily when the birds sat on them.

Fertilizers used on the land to increase the growth of crops eventually change the balance of the soil. As a result, many wild flowers die, and so do many butterflies and insects which feed on the flowers.

Pollution from industry is another threat. Sulphurous fumes are discharged into the air from factory chimneys and carried many hundreds of miles away, where they condense into acid rain. Trees in Scandinavia are dying as a result of acid rain which originates in the heavily concentrated industries of Britain and Germany. The effects of acid rain are spreading to other parts of Europe and also here in the United States. Germany is now spending vast amounts of money trying to reduce the sulphur level in smoke emitted from factory chimneys.

In Europe, fertilizers are now generally being used more sparingly, and the most lethal pesticides have been banned.

robin

With the disappearance of forests, many woodland creatures adapted to live in hedgerows. But now these are being destroyed, and with them the last refuges of many plants and animals.

song thrush

Bats harm nobody. But now they are becoming rare. Old trees and old houses are being destroyed, leaving them without enough places to roost. In Britain it is now illegal to kill bats, even if they roost in your house.

a bat roosting

Butterflies have become rare where insecticides are used. Many of the plants on which they live are also killed, either directly by herbicides, or because fertilizers are changing the chemical balance of the soil. Here you can see a butterfly which has been caught by a hunting spider lurking in the flower.

bugle flower

hunting spider

peacock butterfly

Cool grasslands

Vast areas of grassland are found in the dry interiors of continents. Here rainfall is insufficient for trees to thrive, and the unvaried scenery consists mostly of a flat expanse of grass. Grasslands do not support a great variety of animals, although those that do, occur in enormous numbers.

The prairies of North America were once typical grasslands, although they have now been changed out of recognition by farming and cattle-raising.

These animals had adapted to living in the open without cover, and evolved their own ways of surviving and escaping danger.

The smaller animals, like the prairie dogs, lived in burrows underground where they were hidden from view. The pronghorn antelopes relied on speed to escape their enemies, and were among the fastest runners in the world. Bison used to congregate in enormous herds, finding their safety in their size and their numbers.

With no trees or dense vegetation, the hunting animals could not hide and ambush their prey. Instead they relied on speed and co-operation. Wolf packs, for example, chased their prey as a team. They took turns to lead the chase until the victim was exhausted and the pack caught up.

Recently, the grasslands have been

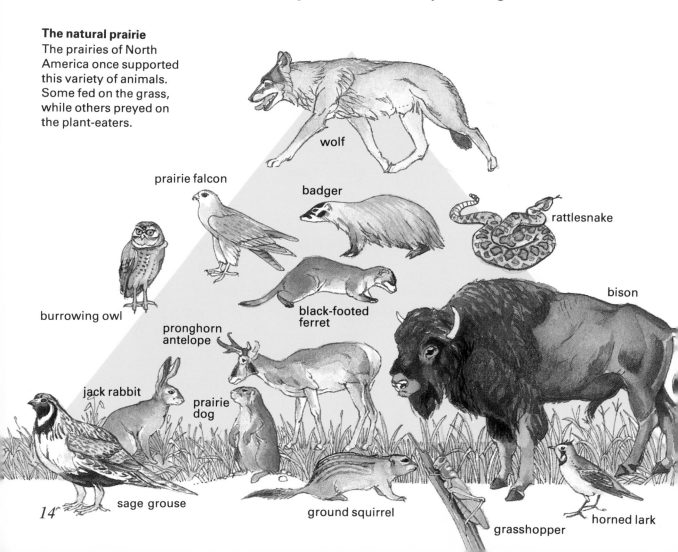

The natural prairie
The prairies of North America once supported this variety of animals. Some fed on the grass, while others preyed on the plant-eaters.

wolf

prairie falcon

badger

rattlesnake

burrowing owl

black-footed ferret

bison

pronghorn antelope

jack rabbit

prairie dog

sage grouse

ground squirrel

grasshopper

horned lark

almost entirely taken over for human use, and the wild grass has been largely replaced by cereal crops. People rely on these crops (which are varieties of grass) for food. Wheat, rye, barley, and maize are an important part of our diet. On the western prairie, where it is too dry to grow crops, the land is used for cattle-raising.

The prairie dogs have been largely exterminated because horses and cattle often stepped into the dogs' burrows and broke their legs. As a result, the black-footed ferrets, which preyed on the prairie dogs, are now close to extinction.

The bison and pronghorn have gone from the prairies, because they were hunted out. By the end of the last century there were only ninety surviving bison. Both the bison and the pronghorn are now protected in nature reserves and are no longer endangered.

Only the mule deer have benefited. They have moved out from the woodlands to take over the pronghorns' range. In fact the deer have thrived so much that they have become pests in some places.

Sadly, the prairies have been altered to such an extent that the original prairie animals will never be able to return to their grassland homes.

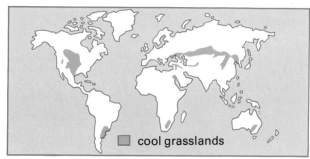

cool grasslands

The effects of people
Now the prairie has been taken by people. It supports cattle in the dryer areas; elsewhere the natural grass has been replaced by cereal crops to feed us and our livestock. Very few of the original grassland animals have survived.

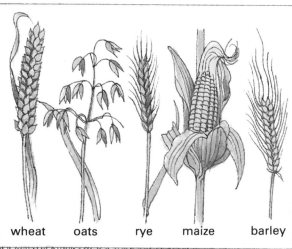

wheat   oats   rye   maize   barley

Savannahs

Hot tropical grasslands are called savannahs. These are vast expanses of grassland in the interiors of continents, bordered by forest on one side and desert on the other. Unlike the cool grasslands, some savannahs are studded with trees and shrubs, and support a great variety of animal species.

In the savannah of East Africa, for instance, many different grazing and browsing animals live peacefully together. Although they are all herbivores they do not compete with each other for food.

Zebras eat the coarse grass-heads, wildebeest eat the leafy centers, while gazelles graze on the base of the grass. The long-necked giraffes find food on the highest branches of the trees. The eland and the black rhinoceros find food lower down on the trees, and the tiny dik-dik browses on the very lowest branches. The white rhinoceros eats grass during the daytime, while the hippopotamus grazes at night, staying in the water during the day to keep cool. Some animals, like the nyala, reedbuck and waterbuck, live near water, while others like the gerenuk and oryx keep mainly to the drier areas.

The predators do not have to compete with each other, either. Lions live and hunt together in the open grassland. The more solitary cheetah relies on speed to run down its prey, while the leopard ambushes its

savannah

Savannah life
The African savannah supports a huge variety of grazing and browsing animals, which live without competing for food. The browsers feed at different heights on the trees. The grazers eat different grasses at different times of the year.

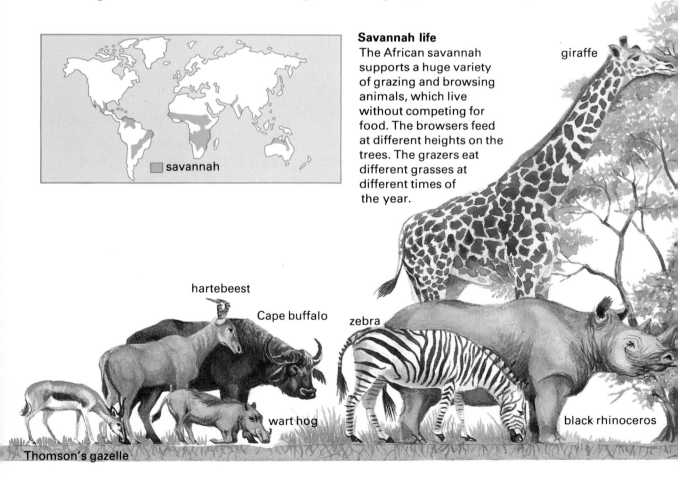

giraffe

hartebeest

Cape buffalo

zebra

wart hog

black rhinoceros

Thomson's gazelle

prey from the cover of the trees and undergrowth, it frequents.

Unfortunately, this perfect natural balance is being rapidly destroyed and the great variety of animals is declining.

In modern Africa, the human population is increasing dramatically, and because Africa is a poor country, with very little industry, cattle-raising and primitive farming are the only means of survival for great numbers of people. And so trees are cut down, mostly for use as firewood for local people, and in the dry areas, cattle overgraze the grass, stripping the land of cover. The occasional droughts in these regions, accelerate this destruction, and may even become permanent as grassland is turned into desert.

Basically, the problem is that there are more people and cattle than the land can support. It has been calculated that the wild savannah animals could provide up to four times as much meat as domestic cattle, and with far less damage to the land. This has now become a real possibility.

As for the wild animals themselves, many are now protected in great reserves, and others still manage to survive in smaller numbers in the wild. They form one of the most amazing natural wonders of the animal world, and it would be tragic if they were lost to us forever.

elephant

eland

gerenuk

wildebeest

Now most of the land is taken for cattle. These overgraze the pasture and destroy the ground cover. With drought, frequent in Africa, the land erodes and becomes desert.

Deserts

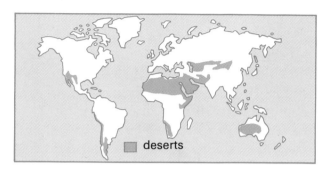

Deserts are one of the most inhospitable regions of the world, although they are not all sand-covered wastes. Some deserts, like the Gobi in Asia, are cold for much of the year. But most deserts are found in the tropics. The main difficulties of life in these deserts are to get enough water and to withstand the intense heat of the day.

Some plants avoid times of drought by growing only when rain falls, then quickly dying and leaving seeds for the next fall of rain. Some, like cacti, store water in their leaves, and others store water in bulbs and tubers underground. The few trees survive by sending their roots far down into the soil to tap underground water.

The arid deserts blossom spectacularly when rain does fall. Dormant seeds of many annual flowers burst into life.

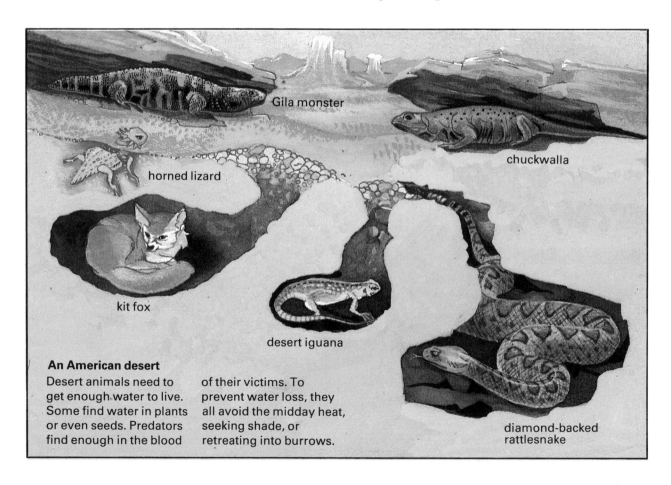

Gila monster

chuckwalla

horned lizard

kit fox

desert iguana

diamond-backed rattlesnake

An American desert

Desert animals need to get enough water to live. Some find water in plants or even seeds. Predators find enough in the blood of their victims. To prevent water loss, they all avoid the midday heat, seeking shade, or retreating into burrows.

Animals have also had to adapt in order to withstand drought. Many insects complete their whole life cycle during one of the infrequent rainfalls. The next generation survives as eggs and pupae until it rains again. Amphibians, like frogs and toads, rest underground during the dry season, having completed the three stages of their development, from egg to tadpole to adult, during the brief rainy season.

Reptiles, like snakes and lizards, are well-adapted to the desert. They hatch as miniature adults and therefore do not have to go through the dangerous tadpole stage. Their scaled waterproof skins prevent them from losing moisture through their bodies. Lizards thrive, and are the most commonly seen animals in the desert.

Mammals that live in the desert only survive by conserving the limited amounts of water they can find. The most famous is the camel, which stores fat in its hump. When no water is available, the fat is digested to produce hydrogen. This combines with the oxygen it breathes in to produce water (a mixture of hydrogen and oxygen). When camels do find water they drink up to twenty-four gallons at a time.

Small rodents like kangaroo rats, drink no water at all. They rely on the low water content of the seeds they eat, added to the water produced by their digestive systems.

Most birds have not had to adapt specially to life in the desert. Their ability to fly enables them to cover long distances swiftly to find sources of water.

For centuries, the deserts of the world were impenetrable, except for the few nomadic tribes living there. But in recent years, deserts have been found to be a rich source of oil. The oil industry has brought more people into desert areas, and modern cars and guns have made it easy for people to hunt the wild animals. As a result, many of the larger desert animals have been hunted to near extinction.

Although irrigation has transformed a few areas to fertile farmland, we cannot change the desert. In fact, rather than destroying deserts we are actually creating more desert. In marginal, or semi-desert, over-grazing by domestic cattle destroys what little is left of the vegetation. And when there isn't enough grass to cover the ground, it becomes desert. The land is then largely useless to humans although it provides a new home for desert animals.

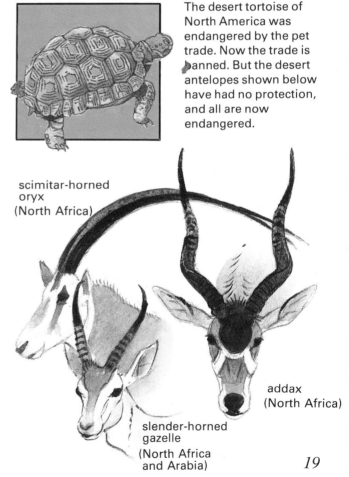

The desert tortoise of North America was endangered by the pet trade. Now the trade is banned. But the desert antelopes shown below have had no protection, and all are now endangered.

scimitar-horned oryx (North Africa)

addax (North Africa)

slender-horned gazelle (North Africa and Arabia)

The rain forests (1)

The tropical rain forests are unique because they support the greatest variety of plant and animal life in the world.

Near the equator, where the forests are situated, the weather is always warm and there is rainfall all the year round. These are ideal conditions for plant growth. Vast numbers of different kinds of trees grow in the forests. Tall trees tower above the rest, with smaller varieties packed between. Beneath these, in what is called the under-story, are even smaller varieties which live in the gloomy shadows.

The soil is shallow because the fallen leaves swiftly rot and provide nourishment for the growing trees. Although plant life is very varied, not many small plants grow on the forest floor, because little light can penetrate the dense jungle. Vines called lianas grow from the ground, climbing the trees to flower in the light. Beautiful orchids and other exotic plants grow on branches,

having no contact with the ground at all but catching rain water as it falls.

Most of the animal life is concentrated in the trees. Birds of prey nest in the tallest branches. Below them, in the canopy of treetops, there are monkeys, squirrels, sloths, snakes and many colorful and exquisitely-plumed birds, as well as a vast host of insects. To many animals, the ground is no more than a highway between trees, but there are also some animals which live only on the ground. In South America, the ground-dwelling tapirs and capybara, and the jaguars which prey on them, haunt the numerous rivers there.

All the animals are permanent residents in the forest. As the plants and trees grow, flower and bear fruit throughout the year, the animals have no need to migrate. But people have begun to exploit the forests on a large scale, and some of the animals are already threatened.

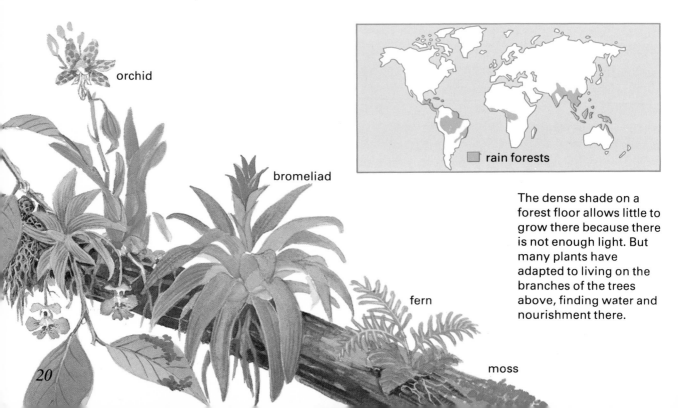

orchid

bromeliad

fern

moss

rain forests

The dense shade on a forest floor allows little to grow there because there is not enough light. But many plants have adapted to living on the branches of the trees above, finding water and nourishment there.

emergent trees

canopy layer

understory

shrub layer

forest floor

A forest section
Tropical forests can be divided into layers. Few animals live in the emergent trees or on the ground. Most are concentrated between the canopy and the understory of the forest. The picture shows the layers in a South American forest, and some of the huge variety of animals living there.

swift

lesser anteater

marmoset

toucan

emerald tree boa

morphos butterfly

iguana

humming bird

spider monkey

arrow frog

jaguar

tapir

leech

hercules beetle

The rain forests (2)

People have lived in the rain forests for a very long time, but it is only recently that they have caused any extensive damage to the environment. The tribesmen who still inhabit the forests, tend small 'gardens' in the interior, and carry on the same traditional way of life as their ancestors before them. Their agricultural methods are primitive and do no harm to the forest.

They make a clearing by felling trees. The trees are then burnt and the ash provides fertilizer for the soil. Then crops are planted. These include sweet potatoes, sugar cane, bananas, pumpkin and water melon. After a few seasons, the soil is exhausted and nothing more will grow. So the clearing is abandoned and a new garden is made. Because the abandoned clearings are surrounded by trees, new trees can seed there and the forest can regenerate itself.

But nowadays, the forests are being invaded by people who use them in a different and far more damaging way. The hardwood trees in the rain forests are highly valued by the timber trade. Consequently, huge areas of the forest are felled from the edge of the forest into the interior. Settlers then follow the trails of the tree-loggers, cutting down more trees to farm the land, and moving on again when the land has become useless. When the land is no longer surrounded by forest, it cannot recover. The soil bakes into laterite, a substance hard enough to build a house with, and the cleared area turns into semi-desert where nothing can grow.

In South America, and in other parts of the world, the forests are being destroyed at the rate of over 98 acres a minute. Many plants and animals perish along with the forests. In Africa, for instance, gorillas have

South American Indians make small gardens in the forest. They cut the trees and burn them, using the ash for fertilizer. When the garden stops yielding they move on to clear another patch, allowing the forest to recover.

Modern technology can clear great areas of forest very swiftly, and on such a scale that the forest cannot recover. Roads, like the ones through the Amazon, are not a danger in themselves, but are damaging because so much more forest is opened up for development.

become threatened, and only survive in a few remote areas. The same fate has befallen the orangutans in Indonesia, and many monkeys in South America.

The forests support such an immense variety of species, it is thought that there are many plants, and maybe even some animals, which still remain to be discovered. If the forests are destroyed they can never be recreated in their original form, and we will never know what has been lost.

Plants as yet unknown may be used to cultivate new crops to feed a hungry and ever-growing human population. So if we destroy the forests we are not only spoiling the habitat of the wild animals, but we are probably also depriving ourselves of valuable resources for the future.

spider monkey

saki monkey

golden lion marmoset

howler monkey

capuchin monkey

common marmoset

All these new world monkeys and marmosets are forest-dwellers which will not survive if all the forest is cleared.

23

Mountains

As you climb a mountain, it becomes colder and the air becomes thinner the higher you go. Different species of plants have adapted to living at different heights on the mountainside.

On the lower slopes there are deciduous trees, and then conifers. Higher up, there are shrubs, grass and beautiful mountain flowers, called alpines; higher still, the vegetation becomes more sparse, although in summer, shrubs and flowers can still be found in sheltered areas. Finally, the barren ground is only able to support mosses and lichens. The very top of the highest mountains are covered by ice and snow all the year round, and nothing grows there.

Mountain animals have adapted to the cold, the lack of oxygen and the rugged terrain of the mountainside. Sure-footed members of the goat and sheep families live in the mountain ranges across Europe, Asia and America. The mountain lion, or puma, inhabits the mountains of North America; and the Himalayas, north of India, is the home of the fabulous and very rare snow leopard. Mountain-dwelling rodents, like marmots and chinchilla, thrive in great numbers, and these provide food for many birds of prey. Wolves and bears, which have been hunted out in the lowlands, now only survive in some mountainous areas.

The true mountain animals have always been particularly vulnerable to hunters. In the European Alps, for instance, animals like the mouflon (a wild sheep),the ibex and the chamois have all become very rare as a result of over-hunting. These animals are excellent climbers, and instead of hiding from their enemies, they seek out inaccessible crags where predators cannot follow them. But of course this is no defense

Mountains are the true home of many of our most beautiful garden flowers, such as these gentians, which are found in the European Alps.

These mountain goats roam the Rockies in North America. Protected in some areas, in others they are common enough to provide sport for hunters.

against someone with a gun, who can shoot and kill them at a distance. The rare animals are now protected in reserves which have been set up in the mountains.

As one of the most beautiful and spectacular realms in the world, mountains provide pleasure for walkers, climbers and skiers. Although we cannot destroy mountains, we can spoil them by denuding them of the flowers and animals living there. In many parts of the European Alps it is now illegal to pick wild mountain flowers. But more needs to be done to preserve the grandeur of these last wild places.

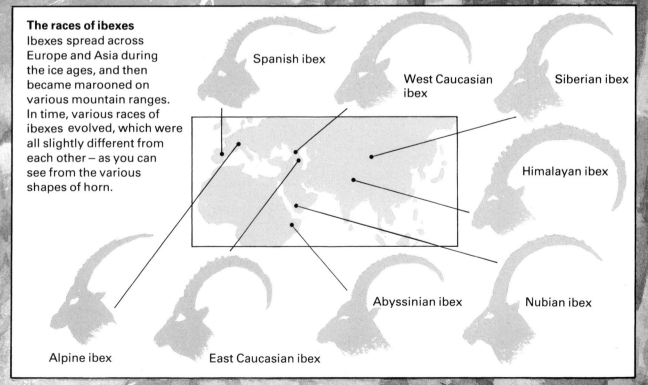

The races of ibexes
Ibexes spread across Europe and Asia during the ice ages, and then became marooned on various mountain ranges. In time, various races of ibexes evolved, which were all slightly different from each other – as you can see from the various shapes of horn.

Spanish ibex

West Caucasian ibex

Siberian ibex

Himalayan ibex

Abyssinian ibex

Nubian ibex

Alpine ibex

East Caucasian ibex

Inland waters

The inland waters of the world support a wide variety of plant and animal life. Fresh water habitats range from running waters of streams and rivers, to the standing waters of ponds, lakes and marshlands.

Animals living in water feed on plants, or prey on other species. Water-dwellers include microscopic animals, shrimps, snails, larval insects and fish. Amphibians, like frogs, newts and salamanders, spend part of their lives in water as tadpoles and as eggs, and all must return there to breed. Reptiles, from snakes to crocodiles, hunt in the water, and many birds, like waders and ducks, rely on fresh water for food. Water voles, otters and beavers are among the mammals found in rivers and lakes.

Water is a vulnerable habitat, and few other realms in the world have been more seriously threatened. Humans need a tremendous amount of water for domestic use, for irrigating farmland and for industry. However, if we take too much water, we change the environment of animals which depend on rivers, marshes and lakes for their survival. For instance, when rivers are dammed for reservoirs, the water flow in the river below is reduced, so fewer animals can live there. When water is drawn from deep wells, the underground water level is lowered, and this can cause marshes to dry out. Marshlands are often drained so that the land can be farmed, and in the process the habitat of many birds and animals is completely destroyed.

Pollution is an even greater danger. When rain falls on the land it drains into ditches, streams and rivers. Once chemical

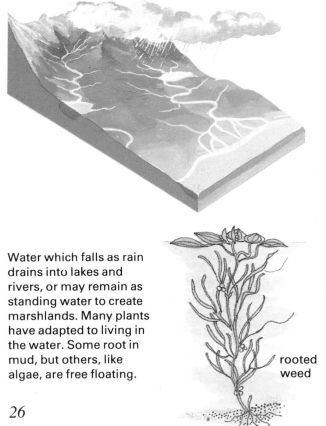

Water which falls as rain drains into lakes and rivers, or may remain as standing water to create marshlands. Many plants have adapted to living in the water. Some root in mud, but others, like algae, are free floating.

rooted weed

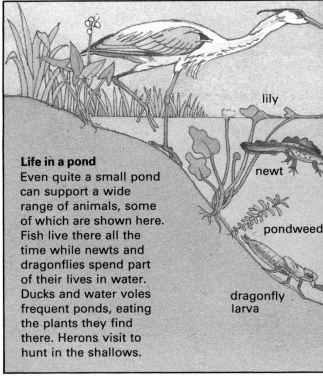

lily

newt

pondweed

dragonfly larva

Life in a pond
Even quite a small pond can support a wide range of animals, some of which are shown here. Fish live there all the time while newts and dragonflies spend part of their lives in water. Ducks and water voles frequent ponds, eating the plants they find there. Herons visit to hunt in the shallows.

substances enter the water they spread very rapidly.

Fertilizers used by farmers to enrich the soil are washed into streams and rivers from the land. The fertilizers often join sewage which is piped into the water. They enrich the water and promote algae growth, seen as cloudy green water. Algae use up so much oxygen that the water becomes unsuitable for fish and tiny water-dwelling animals. Fish-eating birds, like herons and kingfishers, suffer too, because it becomes harder for them to find food.

Pesticides from the land also get washed into rivers. These are persistent poisons which build up in animals and affect the whole food chain, from fish and birds to mammals and eventually to humans. Both pesticides and wastes from industry, which are dumped into water, weaken or kill many animals. Even rain, the source of all fresh water, may be polluted by smoke from factory chimneys.

The damage caused by pollution can be most easily reversed in rivers because the water is constantly flowing. For example, the River Thames in London, England, was lifeless not long ago, but it has been cleaned recently, and salmon, absent for over a hundred years, have been re-introduced.

But in lakes, where the water is still, it is harder to combat pollution. Some lakes are now virtually dead.

Fortunately, water can be purified and life there will return. Water is a necessity of life for all living things, both plant and animal, so it is in our interests to prevent pollution and keep our water pure.

dragonfly

duck

perch

pike

water vole

diving beetle

stickleback

eel

Otters hunt for fish in many different types of waters, but the otters' numbers are declining in many places because of pollution.

Conserving our world

The population of the world is expanding at an enormous rate, and we need more and more houses, roads, factories and farmland to cater for our growing numbers.

A hundred years ago this would not have been considered a problem. Nature was thought of as an inexhaustible wilderness to be tamed and taken over for our own use. But we are now beginning to realize the damage we have caused by the over-hunting of animals, over-use of land, habitat destruction and pollution from industry. As the most powerful species in the world, we have the power to kill or to save wildlife, to destroy or preserve the environment around us. There is no doubt that we have a duty to conserve nature, not only for the sake of the wild animals, but for ourselves.

Ultimately, plants, animals and humans all depend on each other. If we allow plants to survive, they will feed us, and they will feed the animals on which we depend for food. So if we look after the plants and animals, they will help us to survive.

Many thousands of species of animals are threatened with extinction today. For every one species which is saved through nature reserves or captive breeding it is estimated that ten more become endangered.

At least 25,000 plants are threatened, and the oceans and inland waters are becoming so polluted that the extent of damage to marine and freshwater fish is incalculable.

It is a sad fact that many of our most spectacular and appealing animals are in danger of dying out, including the magnificent tiger, many of the great whales, and the lovable koala bear and panda.

purple-stained orchid (Brazil)

birdwing butterfly (Philippine Islands)

golden frog (Panama)

These exotic plants and animals have become rare because they have been collected to be sold. Now they can be protected by law from these trades.

Conservation means ensuring that you are able to wake up and hear birds singing every morning; that you are able to appreciate the beauty of butterflies in your garden and wayside flowers in your road, to look out of the window and see trees; and even if you live in the middle of a large industrial town, to know that you can still go out into wild unspoiled countryside to enjoy the scenery, and marvel at the variety of wildlife around you.

People all over the world, together with governments and conservation organizations are working to preserve the natural environment. You can help, too, by joining a local nature club or one of the larger organizations. If enough people care, it is not too late to save our natural heritage.

bare-headed rock fowl
(West Africa)

A far greater threat to all plants and animals comes from the destruction of their environment as more of the land is taken for human use.

orangutan
(Borneo and
Sumatra)

Index

Illustrated by Maurice Wilson and David Cook